A Kindle Direct Publishing book

Second Edition, October 2019

First Published in 2019

Cover image

Public Domain - View of Crowd at 1963 March on Washington by USIA (NARA)

https://www.flickr.com/photos/39735679@N00/286476887

Creator: U.S. Information Agency. Press and Publications Service. (ca. 1953 - ca. 1978)

To my Mother and Father

The Human Herd

Contents

Preface

 This book attempts to answer some of the big human questions, as well as some smaller ones on the way. It looks at how our instincts as a social animal shape our behaviour and explain some very odd things that humans do.

These instinctive drives act on all of us, but how we react to them varies. Although this book seeks to explain human-wide behaviour, it does not imply that we are all the same, rather that individuals can and do exhibit a broad spectrum of behaviour in response to common instincts. Its message is that by truly understanding and accepting our nature we have the power to change how we behave in an enduring and sustainable way. To do this we need to understand how our instincts drive us; why we are driven to behave in some ways and repelled by other behaviour.

Ideas are presented to help us better understand our nature and so enhance the control we can exert over our lives.

In this second edition a chapter has been added that specifically addresses why it has been so difficult to engage the global population fighting climate change and ways to increase engagement. Links between what we feel and how we act have also been further elucidated as a central conclusion of this book.

Chapter 1

The Human Herd

Humans are a social animal; we love to live in and be part of groups. The cities of the world show this to be true. Socializing with others is a central human experience. This, however, is not unique to humans, there are many social animals, from bees to zebras. For humans, as for other animals, this behaviour is driven by instinct. Humans did not invent living in groups, that behaviour has long existed in the animal kingdom, we just inherited it as part of our evolution.

What is perhaps unique to humans is that we can recognise we have instincts that drive us. With that recognition comes power to control and choose our behaviour. To control we need to understand. With understanding comes power and with power comes choice. To quote a catchphrase of the information age, "information is power". We see this everyday in our ability to create amazing technologies based upon accumulated scientific understanding. These technologies allow us to modify our living conditions on a planetary scale, giving us choice in how we live. The antithesis of this is our seeming powerlessness to prevent large-scale human conflict or act in a rational way to protect the planet upon which we all depend.

In this book I hope to show how some of our basic drives play out in the choices we make. By being aware of these forces our choices can be better informed. I begin this discussion with three basic premises that I accept as true.

(i) That evolution through survival of the fittest is the mechanism that drives how species evolve. No doubt some will argue with this, but to me it is a very well-established idea with overwhelming supporting evidence.

(ii) That humans are a social animal. Firstly, that we are part of the diverse animal kingdom on earth and have evolved from earlier species of animal. Secondly, we are social, that is, we have evolved to live in groups and not as solitary individuals only interacting when strictly necessary.

(iii) That the evolution of our brain structures and thus our behaviours took place in a world full of predators and other threats to our survival. Given the circumstances under which we know humans evolved and our relatively poor physical prowess, that our ancestors were preyed upon and under threat can be taken as fact.

From these premises I hope to show that everything set out below logically follows.

The prime drives in humans are to survive and reproduce. This is a necessary consequence of the mechanism of evolution. By definition, the species characteristics that dominate are ones that are present in the most individuals. Those individuals exist rather than others because their ancestors survived and produced more surviving offspring. So as well as leading to the drive to reproduce, the mechanism of evolution leads to drives that help individuals to produce greater numbers of surviving offspring, that go on to reproduce and survive in greater numbers.

For an animal that lives in groups or herds that are subject to threat, the traits that will be promulgated and become dominant are ones carried by those individuals that survive the threats and control more of the herd's resources related to successful reproduction of themselves and their offspring. So one must first survive, but then be able to access more resources than less successful individuals. For a herd animal the most successful strategy is therefore to ensure your survival by surrounding yourself with the protection of the herd, while garnering as many resources as you can for yourself.

An example I like to use is a herd of zebras being attacked by lions. The individual zebras enhance their chance of survival by staying surrounded by the herd, so they have less chance of being chosen by the lions as prey. For this to be possible a cohesive group must exist and be sustained over time, thus individuals need to act so as to remain part of the herd, that is be a good member who is concerned with the welfare of others. However, individuals within the herd also need to be concerned for themselves above others if they are to optimise their ability to survive.

If the individual zebras had no concern for themselves but were only concerned with the welfare of others (were purely altruistic), every zebra would throw themselves at the lions to be eaten, to protect the other members of their herd. On the other hand, if every zebra was just concerned for itself (was purely selfish), the herd would fragment and individuals would lose its protection. At both extremes the survival of the individuals is compromised. *It is only* when there is a balance between cooperative and selfish behaviour that the chance of individual survival is optimised.

It therefore follows that the most successful individuals are ones that keep in balance selfish and cooperative behaviour. By natural extension, the groups that survive most successfully are those where cooperative and selfish behaviours are in balance across the group. This does not mean that each individual has to be balanced in their behaviour at all times, but that the behaviours tend to be balanced over the whole herd. As we know, there are always individuals that tend to be more selfish than cooperative and those that tend to be more altruistic than selfish.

The simple idea that balanced behaviour is optimal for survival of an individual in a herd explains a great deal of human behaviour, on both the macro and micro level. That is, it can explain war, religion and why we live under moral codes, as well as why, as individuals, some things make us feel good and others bad in everyday life.

Evolution through natural selection, as well as shaping muscles, limbs and senses has led to the development of brain structures that shape behaviour being passed from generation to generation. In animals we call the output of these structures instincts. As we are also animals, we also possess such instincts. A subset of these I call herd instincts. I could call them group instincts or social instincts, but I think that language works to hide their true nature and source. In this discussion it is important to remind ourselves that we are animals that have opposing thumbs and have developed sophisticated communication systems and tools, but still animals at our core. By naming these herd instincts we are overtly reminded of their origin and that, unless we choose otherwise, we have as much control over them as a zebra.

Our instincts, including herd instincts, drive us to behave in certain ways. The instincts express themselves as needs. Our emotion, how we feel in response to a situation, is the thing that drives our behaviour to satisfy the needs. Emotional response is both the reward and deterrent that shapes our behaviour. We tend to seek out things that make us feel good and avoid things that make us feel bad. The stronger the emotion the more we want to engage in or avoid a behaviour.

How we respond to a situation depends upon the structure of our brain, which is determined by a combination of how our genes formed it and the memories we have accumulated. It is after all the connections in our brain that generates the emotions and thoughts upon which we act. The brain structure we have when born provides as close as we can get to pure instinctive responses. This structure is modified over time as memories are laid down. The memories change our behaviour as we learn. What does not change is our pursuit of doing what makes us feel better and avoiding what makes us feel worse. We use our memories to predict how we and the outside world will respond to a behaviour and use that prediction to attempt to illicit responses that make us feel good, or at least avoid feeling bad. It is instincts that dictate our emotions and memories that help us predict how to behave to generate the emotions we seek. Our strongest memories, the ones that most influence our behaviour, are those associated with the strongest emotion. We strongly want to repeat behaviours that made us feel really good and avoid at all costs behaviours that made us feel really bad. Thus instinct drives behaviour via emotion, with memory informing how to behave to achieve the most positive emotional outcome. The more strongly instinctive needs are satisfied, the greater the emotional reward or punishment and thus the stronger reinforcement or avoidance of that behaviour.

An important hypothesis posited here is that behaviours that are able to simultaneously satisfy more than one instinct result in a stronger emotional response and thus stronger reinforcement of the behaviour. The better aligned a behaviour is with our instinctive needs the better we feel, so if a behaviour simultaneously satisfies many needs and satisfies them strongly, we will feel really good and want to repeat that behaviour.

I also posit that it is the overall emotional response that drives behaviour. A behaviour may strongly satisfy some instinctive needs but be contrary others. As long as the overall emotional outcome is positive relative to our current state the desire to carry out the behaviour will be reinforced, as we still feel happier, albeit not as good as when more instincts are satisfied and none dissatisfied. In other words, we need to add up the positive and negative emotions generated by individual instincts in response to a behaviour. If the sum comes out positive, the behaviour makes us feel better and we want to repeat it. If some instincts are satisfied much more strongly than others, those instincts will dominate the outcome. This is why we can continue to do things that seem at odds with some instincts, for example joining the military in the full knowledge that it may lead to our death.

A corollary of these hypotheses is that when there is a choice of possible behaviours, the ones that tend to be chosen are those that most strongly satisfy the most needs simultaneously. Considering this the other way around, to predict which behaviour will tend to be chosen, we simply need to work out which one most strongly satisfies the most needs. I term this the multiple-drives hypothesis. It will be seen in later chapters how this rule explains why some behaviours are much more pervasive than others in human society.

Particularly when we are young, we have insufficient experience to always be able to predict how a behaviour will make us feel, so we experiment, trying out different behaviour, seeing what response we get and how we feel about it. This can be clearly seen in children as they test the limits of behaving selfishly versus being helpful to others. This process is often termed socialization, in other words learning how to successfully be part of the social groups or herds to which we are exposed.

For herd instincts to be satisfied groups (or herds) need to exist. That is, collections of people to whom we can identify as belonging need to exist. If we thought of ourselves as just part of one big group (humanity), the opportunities to compete with others and thus display the balancing selfish behaviours are limited. We cannot compete too strongly with others in our group and still be accepted by them. However, if more than one group exists, we can compete strongly with the opposing group, as we feel no need for their acceptance. Competing against an opposing group also gives us the opportunity to display how strong a member we are of our group. Since competing as groups satisfies multiple needs, it will be a strongly reinforced and thus a pervasive human behaviour. Our instinctive drive to unite with others to be part of a group is thus accompanied by a drive to divide from those not in our group, to reinforce group definition and provide objects of competition.

Herd instincts can operate at many levels and in some ways can be viewed as fractal in nature, that is, no matter at what scale you observe human behaviour, you always see the same patterns. At the smallest group scale an individual lives amongst family and/or friends. Those small groups can also act as individual units in a suburb, city or country, or with shared interest or belief, such as religious or special interest groups. All these groups can behave as individual units, where as a unit they cooperate or compete with other units. Human competition and cooperation extends all the way to the penultimate human scale, where countries of people act as individual units in a collection of such groups that make up the human race. It also extends to the ultimate human scale, that of humanity. At this scale the opposing groups are non-human, such as other animals, insects or bacteria and viruses. Humans also compete and cooperate at this scale, for example competing via the killing of animals for food or to prevent loss of resources we want via habitat clearance, or cooperate by providing such things as animal reserves.

At all these scales it is still the behaviour of individual humans that create the outcome, so the same principles and instincts act at all these scales and the same understanding can be applied to predict and understand behaviour. Thus it is helpful to talk about individual units that act according to these instincts, where an individual unit can be an individual human, a social class, a nation of individuals or those grouped by a common belief system such as adherents to the Catholic Church or Greenpeace.

As discussed above, the more instinctive needs that can be satisfied by a behaviour, the stronger the drive to manifest that behaviour will be. The simultaneous satisfaction of multiple instinctive drives can be difficult to see when only looking within one scale. For example, as an individual it is difficult to behave selfishly to the people around you while simultaneously cooperating with them. However, when behaviour is manifest over different scales it is much easier to behave selfishly and cooperatively at the same time. For example in team sport you cooperate with your team members to win against an opposing team. So an individual can satisfy their need to cooperate to gain the acceptance of the team and supporters, while simultaneously satisfying their drive to out compete other individual units. Thus engagement in sport tends to be a pervasive human behaviour. War is another situation where multiple needs are simultaneously satisfied and often with the highest emotional content, hence the pervasiveness of wars in human culture and history. Realising this is the case, it is apparent why engaging in these parts of the human experience is associated with strong emotional responses, both elation and despair. I discuss these aspects of human behaviour further in later chapters.

As a shorthand, I refer to the ideas above collectively as the herdism theory. This term will be used throughout the book to describe this hypothesis. I will first more fully introduce the concepts and in later chapters explore aspects of human behaviour, show how they are driven by instincts associated with being a herd animal and use that understanding to answer questions humanity often asks (and some they often don't but should). Firstly, let us examine the drives that result from our herd instincts in more detail.

Chapter 2

Herdism Drives

Our instincts exist because they helped our ancestors survive and have more surviving offspring than individuals without those instincts. In order to do this, the instincts needed to be expressed as behaviours by the individual. If the instincts were not expressed they would have no impact in the physical world. Thus for instincts to be useful in an evolutionary sense a mechanism to convert them to behaviour is required. Emotion is this mechanism, conferring emotional rewards for behaviours consistent with our instincts and emotional punishment for those that are inconsistent. In general we are driven to do things that make us feel good and to avoid doing things that make us feel bad. As with other instincts, we thus feel good if we behave in ways consistent with our herd instincts. The main drives associated our herd instincts are discussed below.

The drive for acceptance
Herd instinct creates in us a craving for acceptance by others that we define to be part of the group or groups to which we want to belong,

particularly groups that we perceive can protect us from threat. This typically starts in childhood with our family group. Gaining parental acceptance is a strong need for most individuals, as in childhood they are our primary protection against threat and in turn our parents are driven to protect us as the vehicle for their genes. For many children this drive decreases in strength with age, as other sources of protection become preeminent. To the parents however, they continue to have the same importance as bearers of their genes, thus the parent's drive to protect their children tends not to decrease as they age.

Protection from predatory threat at any age does not only stem from the immediate family group. Being part of a larger group can lower the chance that one will be individually threatened rather than other members. This is a natural consequence of predatory threats being finite and so not able to target all individuals simultaneously. That is, a lion can only eat one human at a time. Thus we are also driven to be accepted by larger groups, for example a group of friends, supporters of a sporting team, adherents to a religion or religious sect, nationality, ethic group, human rights campaigners, animal rights campaigners, the military or fighters for peace or the environment, to name just a few of the almost infinite number that humans have constructed.

Our herd instincts thus result in a drive for acceptance and inclusion; to know that others have our back and that we do not need to face life's threats alone. This instinct is the source of the common experience of feeling like you are "part of something larger", accompanied by feelings of strength and purpose when engaging in shared activities with goals that are clearly stated and shared. These feelings tend to be more intense the larger the group, its singleness of purpose and the stronger any external threat is perceived to be.

The drive to divide

The drive to be accepted as part of a group means we are also driven to define the group to which we belong. To do this we must define those who do not belong to our group. The scale of the group depends upon the scale at which any threat or reward, perceived or real, applies. For example, avoiding the threat of starvation though poverty will often apply at the level of a family group, where the family's access to resources is important. For this threat, the family group is the one that we are driven to maintain and thus we define ourselves as part of the family and deserving of some of its food. If the threat is of war with another country, the relevant group we seek to define is based on nationality, which is distinct from the nationality of the enemy. The ultimate group for humans is humanity, where all humanity is equally threatened. In this case we would define ourselves as human, distinct from other non-human species (such as a pandemic virus). At any scale, without a definition of who is and who is not in your group, there can be no distinct group. This drives us to divide ourselves from those we define to be not one of us.

The existence of other groups also provides someone to compete with, where the competition is sanctioned by our herd as we are defending it or fighting for it. In this instance the need to compete therefore does not conflict with the need to cooperate.

Using the principle that the more needs that are satisfied the stronger the behaviour manifestation, the drive to divide is naturally stronger than the drive to unite. The drive to unite satisfies only our need to cooperate to maintain a cohesive group and be accepted by them. The drive to divide also satisfies this need, as it helps us to define our group, however, it also satisfies our need to be selfish and compete with others for resources, where in this case we compete as the group. The drive to divide is thus intrinsically stronger that the drive to unite. This explains why humans seem to have to work much harder to get groups to cooperate than they do to get them to compete. Seen in the light of herd instinct, where the strength of the drive is equated to the number of needs satisfied, this is a logical consequence of our evolved survival strategies.

Of course, the drive to unite and the drive to divide will always be in tension. If there is a large and powerful threat the drive to unite will tend to win over the drive to divide, as the source of threat provides the opposing group and the larger and more cohesive our group the better the protection. For example when a foreign country wages war on another the cohesion of both societies increase and the drive to unite wins out. When perceived threats are low and thus protection of a large herd not so required, the drive to divide will tend to win.

The drive for prestige

The drive for individual reproductive success leaves us with a need to maximise our own prestige within a group, so that we can garner for ourselves and our offspring as much of the group's resources and protection we can (including the best sexual partner(s)). In a group context, gaining prestige is a more effective method for obtaining resources than overt selfish behaviour, such as theft. Being a prestigious member of a group tends to cement the individual's place within it, whereas overt selfish behaviour tends to result in the individual being shunned by the group. Put more simply, if you have prestige the group will give you extra resources and protection, if you just try to grab them you risk both the resources and the protection of the group being withdrawn.

A group confers prestige upon an individual. Indeed, outside the context of a group prestige is a meaningless concept, as our prestige is how others think and feel about us. The prestige of an individual will be high if the group's collective opinion is that the individual can enhance the survival of the individuals in the group, either directly or through increasing the group's prestige. To gain and maintain prestige, the individual can be seen to act in the best interests of the group and will often be driven to do so by their drive for acceptance. Prestige can also be conferred if someone has achieved a position that we desire, that is, they are perceived to be successful according to the group norms. So becoming a prestigious individual can satisfy multiple needs simultaneously, the need to be accepted, the need to cooperate and the need to maximise their share of resources. This is why success via prestige is a more prevalent human behaviour that an overt grab for resources such as theft or theft with violence. To maintain their position in the group, an individual must balance desire for resources (commonly termed greed) with the cooperative behaviours that underlie their prestige.

The same drive operates at different scales. For example, the prestige (and therefore share of resources) of a country or religious group are sought to be maximised in the same way as an individual within a group may seek to maximise their prestige. For an individual seeking to raise the prestige of their group this can be a particularly powerful drive, as they can be rewarded emotionally for their allegiance to the group and by competing successfully within their own group and against other groups, increasing the group's resources and thus their own in the process.

The drive for resources

This is not strictly a herd instinct, as it will also act on non-social animals, but is nonetheless a strong drive that is important to understand in how it relates to herd instincts. Everyday experience suggests that humans seek to increase their net resources, that is, use as little of their existing resources as possible to gain as many new resources as they can. In short, get the maximum return for the minimum effort. Thus when considering this drive it is important to consider the drive to accumulate in concert with the drive to expend the minimum effort to do so. In evolutionary terms it does not make sense to engage in behaviours that might result in an increase in personal resources, if it is so hard to get them that you die in the process. Thus humans are generally not driven to work harder than they need to to gain the resources they seek. This is another reason why humans are driven to be part of a group. As well as gaining protection, being part of a group can greatly magnify the efforts of an individual, thus increasing the return gained for the effort expended.

The drive for balance

As discussed above, the survival of individuals within a herd is optimised if a balance is maintained between competitive and cooperative behaviours. We are thus driven to try to obtain a balance within ourselves and within the group. For individuals seeking to balance their own behaviour this is often called "having a conscience", or referred to as the battle between good and evil within us. The drive for balance within a group is manifest in the concept of fairness. Humans are often subject to righteous indignation if they feel that they, or someone else, is being treated unfairly by others. The sense of unfairness can arise from individuals or groups not being treated as well as we think they should be, that is, they are subject to what is perceived to be excessively selfish behaviour by others. Additionally, we perceive it as unfair if individuals are being treated too well, that is, not receiving the punishment they should for displaying excessively selfish behaviour or gaining more resources than their prestige dictates they should. Thus feelings of fairness or unfairness are an expression of our instinctive drive to keep selfish and cooperative behaviours in balance.

In the following chapters I discuss how these drives relate to common human experience.

Chapter 3

The Role of Diversity

Evolution requires diversity. Diversity presents options that can be selected through environmental pressures. Without diversity adaption through natural selection will not function. This is just as true for behavioural responses as it is for physical attributes. Although the same instinctive drives exist across all humanity, how they manifest in behaviour is quite variable. For individuals, how their brain is wired will determine how they respond to a situation. That wiring is a result of genetic factors and past experience. Each person's brain starts with a basic structure that is built via their genes. This structure is modified over time as experiences are converted into memories, where the response to the memories is informed by the existing brain structure. Since each of us has a unique combination of starting brain structure and experience history we will also have a unique brain structure and thus different responses to the same input stimuli. Thus different behaviours make us feel good or bad. For example, whereas most people may feel most comfortable in a loving supportive environment, some seem to seek out conflict and abusive relationships. The commonality is that we are all behaving in ways that satisfy our needs. I believe one of those needs is to reconcile how we view our self and the world with how the world views and treats us. Successful reconciliation allows our experiences to be predictable and thus we feel better equipped to survive them. The need to reconcile our internal and external views is thus part of our survival instinct.

We each have an internal view of what sort of person we are. We also have a view of what the world is, such as a place where danger lurks in every corner or one where opportunities abound if we are prepared to take them. It is these views we use to predict how others and the world will respond to us. The more accurate the predictions, the better we can behave in ways that we think will maximise our survival.

Our internal view is driven by our brain structure, which is an integration of its starting structure and how past experiences have moulded it. If our present environment differs from the past, how others see us may be very different from how we see ourselves. This occurs because the daily interactions that inform how others see us are in the present, whereas our brain structure is rooted in the past. For example, someone who has come from an abusive childhood, may view themselves as a victim or a worthless person that deserved everything they got. If that person in adulthood finds themselves in a relationship with a loving and supportive partner and a "good" life according to society's norms, the world will view them in a different way from how they see themselves. In the earlier stages of experiencing this change the world will not make sense to the individual, as their brain structure expects abusive responses whereas they experience supportive ones. This creates a perceived survival threat as they can no longer predict and thus control their world. The response to this threat can be that the individual tries desperately to change their world to make it predictable once more, for example by seeking out new abusive relationships or returning to their old ones. The longer that someone experiences a changed environment, the greater the new experiences will modify their brain structure and so the more the new environment makes sense to them. Thus over time individuals will adapt their internal view in a way that makes it more consistent with the world they find themselves in, decreasing the perceived threat. How fast this happens depends upon the strength and age of the past memories. The stronger the emotion associated with a memory and the more it has been reinforced over time the stronger the neural connections will be and so the greater influence it will have on present behaviour; thus traumatic memories, particularly early ones, are the most difficult to counteract with new memories that are more appropriate to the changed environment. This can manifest in such conditions as PTSD, where an individual continues to display behaviour that is seemingly inappropriate for their current situation, because it arises from past traumatic memories that are difficult to counteract.

In short, how we respond to a particular behavioural stimulus will depend upon the structure of our brain at that moment and thus vary person to person, however, what is universally true is that we will tend to respond such that our emotional needs, which are linked to our instinctive drives, are best met, or that we at least seek to minimise our emotional pain, if we can see no way to gain emotional reward.

In my view committing suicide is an example of emotional pain minimisation. Typically, suicidal individuals see little or no effective way to gain emotional reward but are consumed by emotional pain. They feel isolated, alone and worthless, unable to engage with others in a meaningful way. In short, they see no way to satisfy their herd instincts. The only way they see open to them to remove the pain associated with this lack of satisfaction is by ending their life, which is counter to the instinct to survive. For these individuals, at this time, the emotional pain due to the loss of herd instinct satisfaction is so great that it is not sufficiently countered by their survival instinct to prevent them from taking their life.

As well as variation in response between individuals due to genetic and individual experience differences, there is a cultural overlay that guides what is experienced and thus how an individual will tend to behave. The source of authority in different cultures espouse somewhat different group behaviour norms. To be accepted by the cultural group, individuals will behave in line with these norms. So individuals living in different cultures will tend to respond differently to the same stimulus, as they seek to conform to the differing norms. Diversity in response is therefore not only among individuals but also among cultures. As with other aspects of herdism, culture is present on different scales.

After all, culture is really just another name for group norms and groups can be of many different sizes. Cultures can be associated with a race, country or geographic region as well as with a religion, sporting team or family.

Similar to brain structure, culture arises though a combination of the heritage culture of the people in the group (the analogue of the brain's starting structure), the environment in which they now operate and what major events have occurred to the group, such as wars, famines or epidemics (the analogue of traumatic memories). For example, humans migrating to a new area will bring a culture with them, this culture will be modified over time in response to any environmental factors that differ from where they originated and will be changed by any radical events that leave a strong emotional scar on the society. Richard Dawkins in "The Selfish Gene" invented the concept of a meme, which is the cultural equivalent of a gene and spreads through a culture if it better adapts it to the current environment. So over time a culture will evolve in response to local influences. How far it has changed from the heritage culture depends upon how long the human group has been in the environment and what it has had to contend with.

In herd behaviour one of the differences seen at a cultural level is the balance point between competitive and cooperative behaviour. By balance point I mean the balance of behaviour that the culture presents as ideal. Some cultures value the individual more than the group and others the group more than the individual. For example, the culture of the USA is tipped further towards the individual than the culture of Japan. In the USA individuals are taught that you succeed or fail based on individual merit and that you are successful if you outcompete others to gain higher material wealth. In Japanese culture you are successful if you are part of a successful team and that it is important that you know your place in the hierarchy and happily accept it.

Where a culture sits on the spectrum between cooperation and competition is reflected in how equally resources are allocated within the group. In a culture that values competition between individuals more highly, greater income inequality should be expected compared to those that tend to value cooperation and thus sharing of resources. The ratio of the average income for the top 10% of incomes to the bottom 10% of incomes can be used as a measure of resource allocation equality in a culture. According to a UNDP report (Human Development Report 2009, UNDP, accessed on July 30, 2011) in 2011 this ratio was 18.5 for the USA and 4.5 for Japan with Australia (my culture) in the middle at 12.5. The median ratio for the world was 12.3. By this measure there is a large disparity in income equality between the USA and Japan, reflecting the cultural difference in how they value cooperative versus competitive behaviour.

All this diversity means that herdism is useful in providing a framework within which behaviours can be understood and in predicting overall patterns, however, it needs to be recognised that within this framework there is a high degree of variation in how an individual will tend to behave, depending upon personal and cultural factors. In this discussion I attempt to focus on the common themes resulting from our instinctive drives, rather than how a particular individual or culture will respond to those drives.

In the following chapters I explore aspects of human behaviour that I see as being driven by herd instincts. Where appropriate, each chapter starts with a question, then proceeds to show how herdism provides an answer.

Chapter 4

Fashion

Why do we spend so many resources on fashion, when it has no obvious direct link to our chance of survival?

In this context I am taking fashion to be confined to how we look and what we wear. Fashion in the broader sense also includes how we behave, what we profess to believe, what games we play and a myriad of other things that make up the norms of a society. The discussion below equally applies to fashion in the broader sense, but I have chosen to confine it to the narrower view for the sake of clarity.

Fashion, that is dressing in a particular style, of itself does nothing to enhance the chances of survival or reproductive success of individuals. Wearing fashionable clothes (rather than last year's fashions) does not necessarily protect you better from the cold or ensure you give birth more easily for example. Why then is fashion such a strong force, where humans expend huge resources in pursuit of both the creation of and adherence to fashion?

This is one of the more obvious manifestations of our herd instincts, as the overt aim of following fashions is to conform to herd or group norms. The fashion industry is used as a source of authority on how one should look and how one should behave, with the aim of not only being accepted by the group but also as a path to higher prestige. As with other pervasive and long lasting patterns of human behaviour, fashion satisfies multiple instinctive drives simultaneously. Most obviously, by being fashionable an individual can demonstrate their allegiance to the herd, showing they are prepared to look a particular way, no matter how bizarre and impractical that may be, in order to reinforce herd norms and thus increase herd cohesion. The drive to divide is also satisfied, as we conform to a particular fashion sub-group and use how we look as a very obvious way of distinguishing ourselves from those in other fashion sub-groups. Fashion also gives the individual a strong platform for competing with others within their group. Part of the essence of being fashionable is to be "on trend", that is, aligned with the current group norms or even better, seen to be displaying emerging norms. You are seen as more fashionable than others if you are better at discerning the emerging trends, and thus more attuned to the group. Thirdly, fashion is a vehicle for an individual to increase their prestige. The ability to keep up with fashion traditionally is in part dictated by how many resources you control (i.e. how much money you have to be able to afford the latest look). The most fashionable are thus associated with having access to greater resources and "being in the know", so tend to have higher prestige. It is no coincidence that, at least in mainstream western society, more fashionable and more expensive go hand in hand. "Paying for a label" is a common experience for many. If a strong adherence to fashion can also be combined with an increase in sexual attractiveness, the drive to couple and reproduce with the "best" partner also drives the behaviours. One of the aims of being fashionable is to increase your sexual as well as social prestige, in the hope that this will be recognised by potential mates, attracting one with higher prestige. This is a particularly strong drive for the young. They have the longest reproductive life ahead of them to profit from any advantages they can derive from being fashionable. Thus in fashion terms, the ultimate is to be young, rich, on trend and sexually attractive, as these people are most strongly satisfying the largest number of instinctive drives and are thus seen as something that should be aspired to. This explains the "Paris Hilton" phenomenon, where huge prestige is conferred upon an individual that displays these characteristics.

Fashion is an example of how the power to make positive change can be derived from understanding why we feel driven to behave in the ways we do. Without understanding, a huge amount of human effort and the planet's resources is spent on fashion, driven by our instincts. If we understand that this is happening we can choose other ways to satisfy these drives that are less resource hungry, which is better for us, as we have more resources for other things and better for the planet we rely on.

Chapter 5

Sport

Why do humans seem to be so fascinated by sport?

As with fashion, humans spend a disproportionate amount of their resources on sport. This cannot be purely explained as participation in sport being practice to hone survival skills, as spectators rather than participants increasingly engage in modern sport. Equally, it cannot be explained purely in terms of satisfying a human need for entertainment, as it begs the question of why we find sport so entertaining?

When considered in terms of our herd instincts, sport is a quintessential expression of the human drive for a balance between cooperative and competitive behaviours. Sport is nominally about competition between opposing individuals or groups, but it is only competition within strictly defined sets of rules. Thus in sport we are encouraged to compete with others, but only when done in ways that are sanctioned by the herd. Thus adhering to a sporting code is another way of showing that you are a "good" law abiding member of the herd, while still being a strong competitor and thus a strong and worthwhile member. The strong drive for balance as expressed through sport is shown by the punishments handed out to those who transgress the rules. These punishments vary from a competitive advantage being handed to your opponent in the form of a "free", all the way through to lifetime bans and social vilification, think Tonya Harding and Lance Armstrong. So in sport you should be a strong competitor, but only when that is balanced by playing by the rules. If you don't, competition is out of balance with cooperation, so subverting the essence of sport, thus you get punished.

In sport, if you lose you are largely ignored, but if you lose with good grace you can somewhat redeem yourself. If you win through cheating you are shunned, but if you win within the rules you are glorified. Thus sport glorifies balance. Sport satisfies multiple instinctive drives simultaneously. For participants it satisfies the drive to compete, but to compete in a way that simultaneously leads to acceptance by the group, as you are being seen to follow the group rules while competing. It is thus "guilt free" competition that you can feel good about, as it is officially sanctioned, rather than feeling you are being unfair to others. It also satisfies the drive for prestige, as being a successful sportsperson can greatly elevate your position in society. In sport the elevation in prestige can be within your friendship group, right through to being publicly recognised as "the best in the world". For team sports there is the additional payoff of being part of a group, which allows you to compete, but also cooperate as part of the team. It is no coincidence that "being a team player" is a strong theme in sport or that an ultimate aim for many sportspeople is to be able to compete on behalf of their country. By competing for your country you not only have the opportunity to show yourself as a champion of a very large herd, but also to maximise the impact of your increase in prestige.

For spectators and supporters, their drive to compete can be satisfied vicariously through the sportspeople or teams they follow, as well as by competing with rival groups of supporters, where being a strong competitor is synonymous with behaviour that enhances supporter group cohesion. So, as for participants, society has encouraged supporters of sport to compete with others and feel good about winning, without the nagging doubt that they may be being unfair to the vanquished. If our team wins we are euphoric, as we have successfully competed while simultaneously demonstrating group cohesion and feeling the warmth of shared emotion and experience with others. If our team loses, we comfort ourselves that we played a good game and played by the rules, remaining a loyal member of our supporter group, even in adversity.

The satisfaction of these drives is stronger the larger the stage. The more people involved in the sporting event (usually dominated by supporters rather than participants) the greater the feeling of cohesion and being part of something big. The ultimate expression of this for most people is events like the Olympics or World Cups, where they are supporting one of the largest groups an individual seeks to be part of, their nation. This is also true for the participants, with the added potential benefit that a large stage is often associated with a large amount of money being involved, either prize money or through their increased prestige leading to endorsement contracts, thus satisfying the drive for maximising their net resources.

Chapter 6

Celebrity

Why do celebrities exist and why do we take their opinions so seriously?

In some ways the phenomenon of celebrity is linked to fashion, where one of the herd norms to which we conform is who we designate and follow as a celebrity. However, celebrity in its modern incarnation is a very odd concept. Why do we give such a disproportionately high fraction of society's resources to individuals who appear in the mass media (television and movies) and listen so seriously to their opinion? After all, these individuals may possess skills to act or to entertain us in other ways, but have no more credentials than the average person in the street to comment on other things. In some instances they do not even possess particularly special attributes or skills, but seem to be famous just because they are, for example the Kardashian family or reality TV contestants. Why then do we hang on their words on hunger, world peace, animal rights, gun control or the other myriad topics people with celebrity tend to comment on? Perhaps more starkly, why do we think they are fit to be political leaders, for example Ronald Regan, Arnold Schwarzenegger, Clint Eastwood or Donald Trump?

As with most pervasive phenomenon, there is usually more than one underlying drive being satisfied. In this case one drive could be a by-product of a developed brain that requires constant exercise to maintain optimum function. In a world where more and more of the requirement to think is being transferred to machines and systems someone else has created, the brain still instinctively craves exercise, in this case in the form of entertainment. So part of the reason why we pay movie stars and other celebrities so much is that increasingly they are one of the few ways we have to satisfy the drive to exercise our brains. It is also true that we find the entertainment most satisfying when it engenders a strong emotional response. Since emotions are the reward for drive satisfaction, it is clear that an important role of entertainment is to give us opportunities to vicariously satisfy our instinctive drives.

This, however, does not immediately explain why we tend to take the opinions of celebrities so seriously. I think this is an artefact of the drive for herd cohesion, with its accompanying need for a shared view. We are programmed to want to have a shared view with those around us, to gain their acceptance. Before mass communications this shared view was sourced from the leaders of the group, for example the elders of a tribe, the local government officials or the king of a country. The source of those shared views was looked to as a source of authority, telling us what we should believe to be part of the group. In this situation the people that everyone recognised were the leaders, those that you should listen to if you want to be accepted by the group. Thus if everybody knew about someone they must be important. With the advent of mass media, the individuals that everyone knows and talks about are those we all see via those media. Because everyone knows and is talking about the people they have seen, the evolved wiring in our brain interprets the opinions of these celebrities as a source of authority and the people as important individuals that should be taken seriously. Put simply, modern celebrity is an artefact of previously useful brain wiring that has not adapted to the presence of mass media.

Celebrities as a source of authority are particularly powerful in a world where a traditional source of authority, the religion to which we belong, is disappearing as a force in our lives. This leaves a vacuum in where to look for guidance on what we should believe and how we should behave to ensure acceptance by the herd. In the absence of an external authority humans look to each other for guidance, taking the stance, "if I behave like everyone else and believe what others believe I will be accepted". However, if everyone just looks to everyone else, the rules will be constantly shifting and variable, leading to fragmentation of the herd. A source of information that can be accessed and accepted by all the group members is the best way to promote cohesion. The increasing universality of mass media plays well into the space left by the disappearance in religious belief.

I discuss the need for authority and religion more fully in later chapters.

Chapter 7

Crime

Why is crime against individuals ever-present but so rare that most of us have little personal experience of it?

The low prevalence of crime against individuals is a result of our herd instincts. A crime, by definition, is a breach of the herd rules. When committed against an individual is has the aim of satisfying the needs of the criminal without regard for the victim. Thus criminality, at least by one individual against another, only tends to satisfy the need to compete and in the case of property crime to gain extra resources. However, this behaviour puts the individual at odds with the need to be accepted by society. For most individuals in most situations this is too high a price to pay, so they will only commit what are perceived to be minor crimes that they are unlikely to be caught at, such as not paying fares on public transport or speeding. There is a wide range of reasons for those that commit more serious crimes. This is beyond the scope of this book, except to say, for the behaviour to be sustained there must be a net positive emotional payoff for the criminal. The strongly competitive nature of committing a crime can be offset not only by an increase in net resources for the criminal, but also by it resulting in acceptance by a group such as a family where crime is condoned or belonging to a criminal gang or organisation. In this way criminals can satisfy their drive for herd acceptance.

Looked at in this manner, it is apparent why jails exist as a punishment for crime. By putting criminals in jail, we are strongly isolating them from society and very clearly demonstrating the lack of acceptance of them by the herd, with the most extreme transgressors being placed in maximum security prisons with increased isolation or ultimately, solitary confinement for those individuals that continue to break the rules. If this rejection by society were not a strong disincentive to break the rules, jail would objectively be a desirable place to be for many. Even though they may not have access to partners with which to reproduce, their access to shelter, food and security would be improved in jail compared to their situation outside of jail.

A criticism often levelled at incarceration as a punishment for crime is that you risk turning one-time offenders into career criminals. In light of herdism this makes sense. Individuals that commit a crime are punished by isolating them in jail, strongly demonstrating that they are rejected by "law abiding" society. Thus those individuals will tend to crave group acceptance to make up for the deficit. The group they are immediately exposed to in jail is one where criminal behaviour is more acceptable than in society as a whole. Thus the need for acceptance will tend to drive them to conform to the norms of the group they are exposed to and thus see criminal behaviour as more acceptable than they otherwise would.

Committing a crime is a behaviour that is out of balance in herdism terms (except perhaps when the crime is committed as part of an accepting group). At its essence it is purely competitive and if detected will lead to active rejection by the herd at large and possible isolation from the herd. Perversely, this rejection can lead to a reinforcement of the acceptability of criminal behaviour and this, in combination with the common continuing rejection from mainstream society after leaving jail, can lead to high levels of reoffending.

Chapter 8

Leaders and Followers

Why do human groups always end up with leaders and followers?

It is a universal characteristic of humanity that we have leaders and followers, those who give direction and those who take it. This of course acts at many scales and a leader at one scale may be a follower at another. For example a parent can lead their family unit but be a cog in a wheel at work. The need for leadership is a consequence of the need for shared beliefs that act to define a group and to keep it functioning and coherent. For any group to sustainably function, it needs to have shared objectives and rules and engender a sense of belonging in its members. The sense of belonging comes from "having things in common" with the other group members, that is, believing that similar things are important, reacting in similar ways to the same inputs and having shared experiences. Individuals need to know how to behave to demonstrate they have the values and beliefs necessary to gain and maintain acceptance by the group. This is most effectively established when there is a common source of advice on how to behave to which all group members look. Thus, for a group to function it is necessary to have sources of authority that inform the individuals how to behave and what to believe. This is why herds of wild animals and herds of humans all have leaders, for without a leader or other source of authority to coordinate behaviour, a herd of any significant size cannot be sustained.

Common beliefs and behaviours are impossible to maintain without effective and continual communication with group members. Since herd instinct evolved in a world where ideas and beliefs could only be shared by word of mouth or locally observed actions, a strong source of authority was a human leader, where the group members looked to the leader for guidance. In small groups individuals can interact among themselves and with a leader sufficiently well for this to happen. As the size of human settlements grew this was much more difficult, thus hierarchies of leaders were established to spread the word of the appropriate ways to behave. The hierarchy acts as a disseminator of the source of "truth", that is, how to behave to be accepted by the group. This might be local officials in the case of political leadership or bishops, priests and ministers in the case of religious orders. Interestingly, with the rise of mass communication, the need for communication through a hierarchy has diminished, as it is now possible for the words of a single individual to reach millions directly.

Leadership in all its forms and at all scales is thus a mechanism by which shared values and beliefs can be established and maintained to define the group. It is a necessary consequence of the instincts evolution has equipped us with. The need to have leaders and thus followers is deeply rooted within our brain structures, how that leadership behaves however, is highly variable and subject to its environment.

The link we make, perhaps unconsciously, between leadership and herd cohesion is evident in the link that is often made between leadership and protection, particularly at times when the herd feels under external or internal threat. At these times, strong leaders tend to be chosen that the herd perceives will be effective at repelling the threat. If the threat comes from within, that is, factions within the herd, this will be a person that is looked to to neutralise the dissidence, either by active suppression or removal of the need for the dissidents to continue their group disrupting behaviour. If the threat is external, then the leader chosen will tend to be one perceived to be effective in fighting the threat, for example a military person in the case of threatened armed conflict or a strong negotiator in the case of economic threat. The link between leadership and herd protection is a result of the link we instinctively make between being part of a herd and being protected from threat.

In small family and tribal groups, the leader or leaders will be the individuals that others look to for guidance on how to behave as a member of that group. Naturally, the individuals that were listened to most by the most group members became the leaders. So a leader was someone who was widely known and respected or perhaps feared within the group. Thus in the human psyche we associate the importance of an individual with how many people in the group know of them. There is a reason why in the past and today kings and queens make sure their image is on coins that their followers see every day and why political advertising featuring the party leader is so prevalent. The connection between the commonality of knowledge of an individual within a group and the perception of them as a leader made sense in times when communication was only possible locally, as it was when our brain structures were evolving, but can become perverted when mass communication is available.

Particularly with mass communication, words of authority need not come from an individual, they can in fact be anything that communicates what to believe and what opinions to espouse, for example a printed religious text. In the era of mass communication, individuals no longer need to talk to one another to communicate ideas and beliefs. They can be shared through accepting the authority of material presented by the mass media. The more individuals that listen to or read and accept the ideas and values espoused by the media, the more powerful source of authority it becomes. In my opinion this new technological phenomenon has distorted the original instinctive mechanism, leading to some bizarre outcomes such as the modern manifestation of celebrity.

An interesting progression is this regard is the change that is underway in mass communication medium. This started with printed books and newspapers, then progressed to radio, then movies and television and more recently to the Internet. The former were still controlled by a relatively small group of individuals and so fairly easily co-opted for the maintenance of existing hierarchies. The sources of content available on the Internet are much more distributed and varied, so it is much harder to identify what one should believe. This can lead to fragmentation of groups; as the sources of possible authority multiply, so do the number of groups that identify with those sources. So whereas the Internet is often thought of as a unifying medium, where we all have easy access to the thoughts of others, herdism predicts that it will lead to increased division and fragmentation of human society as it fragments the source of authority.

Chapter 9

Good and Evil

Why are "good" and "evil" such universal human concepts?

When taken at face value the concepts of good and evil seem quite simple. As a human you have the choice to behave in either a "good" or "evil" way. But if you start to delve even just a little bit deeper it soon becomes less clear. One person's good is another's evil, it all depends on your perspective. The concepts quickly become impossible to pin down. Take for example the struggle between Islamic State (IS) and more moderate Muslim cultures or the West. Western society view IS as "evil", inflicting pain and suffering upon countless innocent people in the name of a perverted ideology. However, the members of IS see themselves as warriors of Allah, struggling to bring purity, goodness and enlightenment to the world. Willing to give their lives for what they believe. The West views IS as strongly evil, IS view themselves as the only good people.

When viewed through the lens of herd instinct, what we call good and evil are actually just other names for cooperative and selfish behaviour. We associate altruistic behaviour that enhances a group's experience and cohesion as good and perceive behaviour that is designed to enhance your position, or your group's position, to the detriment of others as evil (if you happen to be one of the others). Herdism tells us that optimal survival occurs when "good" and "evil" are kept in balance, as cooperative and self-centred behaviours are both essential for the survival of the individuals in the herd.

Thus in contrast to the usual view of good and evil (that one is good and the other bad), both behaviours should be seen as useful and valid to enhance our survival as individuals and as a species. Either behaviour becomes not useful in enhancing survival when it is out of balance, thus extreme altruism and extreme self-centred behaviours are not useful. When the imperative is optimal survival of individuals in a herd, the very concept of good and evil, with one applauded and the other condemned, is misplaced. Rather, both these types of behaviours should be seen as valid and useful when in balance. Thus the apparent mystery of why evil persists in the world disappears, as the concept of evil as something inherently bad is invalid. "Evil" behaviour is not bad, it is purely an expression of the instincts we all process to optimise the survival of our genes and is required to be present for us to be successful as an individual and a species.

A reason the concept of "evil" is hard to shake is that believing in it simultaneously satisfies several instinctive drives. Branding another individual or group in opposition to us as "evil" allows us to better define our own group as "good" thus promoting cohesion. It simultaneously gives us permission to behave selfishly towards the "evil" individual or group, to enhance our own position relative to theirs. As an individual within a group, promoting the "evil" of other groups also gives us the chance to satisfy our drive for prestige, as if the majority of our group can be convinced that the outsiders are evil, the more we are seen as promoting group cohesion and keeping our group safe from harm.

This behaviour is clearly seen in the political sphere, particularly in nationalist movements such as the "Make America Great" campaign of Donald Trump. This behaviour ticks all the boxes to satisfy many instinctive drives. It creates threats to those that are part of the "American" herd; all those shadowy forces seeking to destroy the greatness of America. It draws sharp lines around who is part of the "American" herd and who is not, by such means as strongly repelling all that are not officially admitted, hence the Mexican border wall, separation of families to deter illegal immigration and travel bans on members of other countries seen as threats. It creates economic threats, where a weak "America" has been taken advantage of by others, hence the trade tariffs imposed against its competitors to defend against their touted economic threat to the herd. It is particularly interesting that some of the first tariffs announced when Trump became President were against its immediate neighbours, Canada and Mexico. It is harder for Americans to view these countries as not strongly related to them, given the geographic proximity, the large Hispanic population of the USA and the similar accent and general culture of Canada (although Canadians may strongly refute this). Thus a strong effort is required to define Mexicans and Canadians as "not American" and a threat. This all helps to create a siege mentality, where group cohesion is increased through fear of largely imagined external threats. The increased cohesion then acts as a psychological balancing force against the overt selfishness of the behaviours of the "American" herd, allowing it to still satisfy the innate need for a balance between cooperative and selfish behaviours.

For Donald Trump as an individual, this also strongly satisfies his instinctive drives. By creating threats and then being seen to create strong defences, he is satisfying his need to promote group cohesion (often termed speaking to his base), compete strongly against those he defines as not part of his group and maximise his personal prestige in the process, by setting himself up as the individual saviour of a country under threat. He can then parley that increase in prestige to an increase in personal wealth, using his position (or former position) to convince others to make him richer.

The sequence of threat creation followed by Trump as saviour is clearly evident in his interactions with Kim Jong-un. First the threat from North Korea's nuclear arsenal was escalated, with rhetoric of him being a madman who was close to or already had the ability to attack the USA with nuclear weapons. With Donald Trump portraying himself as the strong man calling out a madman. Then came the diplomatic Trump, who alone in the world could bring Kim Jong-un to the negotiating table and thus save America from this imminent threat from an evil herd.

The danger in such nationalist campaigns is going too far, to the point where too many question the reality of the threats and start to feel either that their government is not being fair to them, or they are not being fair to the rest of the world. That is, pushing the selfish behaviours too far out of balance with the cooperative behaviours. If this occurs the herd performs an adjustment. In democratic countries this means replacing those in government with ones that are perceived to have a more balanced view and when that option is not available, an uprising against the government.

Chapter 10

Conflict

Why do we find it impossible to abolish conflicts such as war in the otherwise highly cooperative human species?

As a herd animal, optimising your chance of individual survival demands opposing behaviours, so there is internal conflict built into the central core of human survival. At any given moment individuals or more broadly individual units are pulled in opposing directions, to cooperate with others or to be selfish.

The opposing forces play out everyday as individuals act to enhance their own prestige or share of resources within a group or cooperate to enhance the prestige, power and cohesion of the group to which they belong. Which way we choose to behave is often described as the moral choices we make, but where we are in fact just acting out complementary survival behaviours.

For individuals to survive they must be concerned about themselves, for herd animals to optimise their survival they must also be concerned about the strength of their herd. If either element is missing the individual's chance of survival is greatly diminished. Concern of individuals for themselves will necessarily lead to conflict with other individuals concerned about themselves. For example, if someone possesses resources we want, it is typically less effort to take theirs than to create them for ourselves. Thus the drive to maximise our net resources will naturally lead us into conflict with others.

The only way to abolish conflict is to abolish selfish behaviour, however we have seen that doing this in a herd animal will lead to the demise of the herd under external threat. Thus conflict is necessary.

Having established that in a successful herd animal some conflict is necessary, the idea that the strongest behaviours are the ones that most strongly satisfy the most instinctive drives also leads to the conclusion that conflict between individuals should not be a dominant human behaviour. The source of individual conflict is fundamentally the struggle to maximise our own position to the detriment of others, it only satisfies a single herd drive and can lead to active exclusion by the herd with the accompanying emotional punishment of feeling rejection and guilt. It is behaviour out of balance in a herdism sense. Thus, it is more common for individual humans to cooperate than be in conflict, as this can simultaneously satisfy the drive to cooperate, to be accepted and to increase their prestige, thus be gifted more group resources and increased protection. Although listening to the news every night may lead one to conclude that conflict between individuals is a dominant behaviour, the fact that cities of millions of people continue to function and the extent to which we as a species have been able to modify the planet through working together, makes the dominance of cooperative behaviour self-evident. That our news programs tend to be dominated by accounts of conflict speaks to how rare it is. If experiencing conflict were a common everyday experience, such as saying hello to someone on the street, it would not be "news". That fact that conflict is news, where saying hello to a stranger is the street is not, is testament to its rarity in most people's experience.

On an individual level the multiple drives hypothesis therefore predicts the prevalence of cooperative behaviour. However, it also predicts our inability to eliminate war and other conflicts between groups. When groups conflict, the drive to cooperate and the drive to compete can be satisfied simultaneously. When participating in a conflict between groups, individuals are encouraged to feel part of something larger. In the case of war, the appeal to their instinct to act in the group's best interest rather than their own need to be particularly strong, as the consequences to the individual of participation can be catastrophic. Thus the unabashed appeals to fight for "God and Country", the lauding of serving soldiers as special members of society and the extreme efforts of the military to inculcate strong feelings of acceptance and group cohesion through uniform dress and grooming, ritual, immersion in military life, frequent relocation to help break extended family and external friendship ties and the unquestioning acceptance of authority. This all increases the satisfaction of herd instincts, with the military as the sole source of satisfaction, so they can more strongly counter the loss in satisfaction of the instinct to survive.

Thus when conflict is between groups, our instinctive drive to participate is far stronger than our drive to participate in individual conflict. For large scale conflicts such as war, the increased strength is derived both by the fact that the drive to compete, the drive to cooperate and the drive for prestige can all be simultaneously satisfied, but also because they can each be satisfied so strongly. There is no greater conflict of one individual with another than one where the outcome can be death for the loser. It is also hard to envisage any stronger demonstration of an individual's willingness to be part of a group than to agree to put themselves in situations where they might die on behalf of that group. Society further reinforces the emotional rewards for individuals in the military (or terrorist groups for terrorists) by publicly marking them out as very special people who deserve our thanks and praise, thus helping to satisfy the drive for prestige. It is therefore hardly surprising that while instincts govern our behaviour, war and other forms of conflict between groups such as terrorism will always be present in human affairs.

At this point I think it is also useful to return to how the theory of herdism characterises the concepts of good and evil, as in conflicts between groups, the opposing group is often, if not universally characterised as "evil" and your group as "good". If we now replace the terms "evil" and "good" with "selfish" and "cooperative" you can immediately see why the traditional characterisation is so prevalent. It is self-evident to see the opposing group as selfishly trying to take what you have and your own group as participating in the ultimate act of cooperation. The truth is that both sides are being both cooperative and selfish simultaneously and thus all behaving in ways that satisfy their instincts.

The herdism theory explains why religion is so often intimately linked to conflicts between groups. Why so often "God is on our side so we cannot lose", or, as common in modern terrorism, where the overt source of the conflict is given as adherence to a particular religious doctrine. The role of religion in human affairs and how it naturally arises from our herd instincts is discussed in the next chapter.

The herdism theory also explains the success of such things as the Invictus Games in assisting in the rehabilitation of soldiers injured in combat. As previously discussed, the military is constructed to provide a strong satisfaction of the soldier's herd instincts, to convince them to compromise their need for individual survival. It is therefore easy to see how discharge from the military though injury can have a devastating impact. By being injured the individual has not only lost the competition that was the raison d'etre for being a soldier, but also lost being part of the military world, that was a large and powerful way to satisfy their herd instincts. Their injuries can also make it difficult to reengage with life outside of the military, giving them few avenues to fill the void created. Sport is another strong satisfier of our herd instincts. By these ex-soldiers taking part in the Invictus Games they once again have the opportunity to compete and succeed, to be accepted as part of a larger movement made especially for them and to gain prestige from wider society, thus helping to replace the satisfaction of instincts previously provided by the military. This is in contrast to such things as counselling, individually or in small groups as a therapy, which may help an individual reengage with society, but does little to correct the deficit in need satisfaction that occurred upon leaving the military.

Chapter 11

Religion

Why is religion and belief in supernatural Gods such a constant characteristic of being human, but the content of the religion so variable?

If there was indeed a supernatural being or beings communicating absolute truths to humans, as religions espouse, then why does the content of that communication vary from religion to religion? There can after all, by definition, only be one set of absolute truths.

An answer that may be given by someone who believes in a God is that belief in God is ubiquitous because God is real and that the variable religious content is God testing our faith, with the beliefs of religions that disagree with mine being false. This is an internally consistent view, but does not answer the question at all. Since all religions can claim theirs to be the true religion and their God(s) the true God(s), this answer leaves us with the same question. If God is real, why does every religion believe their God is the true one, when by definition all but one must be wrong? Objectively no religion has a greater claim than the next to be the true religion. So this is not a satisfactory answer to the question. It must lie elsewhere.

Each religion is linked to an originating culture. For example the ancient Egyptian culture had their pantheon of Gods, as did the Greeks, the Romans and the Norse, but the Gods were different. The Jews had their single God, which gave rise to the Christian God, the Arab cultures have Allah and the Indian culture Hindu Gods. It is a matter of historical fact that each set of religious beliefs only began in one place at one time, never simultaneously in multiple places. Thus each religion is intimately linked to the culture from which it originated. Since in every instance the origin of a set of religious beliefs is in a particular culture and culture is unquestionably a human construct, it is evident that the religion must have arisen from the culture and thus must logically also be a human construct.

I will repeat that succinctly as I think it is an important conclusion. Each religion has a unique originating culture, culture is by definition a human construct, since each religion grew out of a culture, religion must also be a human construct.

Some might challenge this by saying that this is so because the true God just happened to be revealed to a single human who could only be part of a single culture. But this still does not address the question of why so many different gods and religions exist and have come and gone over human history.

The argument that religion must be a human construct is fairly straightforward and difficult to robustly challenge, so why is it not more widely recognised? The information that the particular religion practiced and the God(s) worshipped is associated with a culture has been available for thousands of years, for as long as groups of humans have been aware of the existence of other cultures. With that information, the conclusion that religion must be a human construct is a small logical step. The fact that nearly all of humanity has been blind to this simple logic for thousands of years speaks to the power of religion to satisfy our instinctive drives and the power those instincts have to control our thoughts. It appears that our need for a supernatural God has blinded us to the almost irrefutable evidence that religion is constructed by humans.

I find this a breathtaking conclusion. The human brain can approach understanding the composition of atoms and contemplate the beginning of the universe. Nearly all of us have the intellectual capacity to understand things that are far more complicated than the thought process it takes to see religion as a human invention. However, this simple logical step has not been taken by so many for so long, rather, huge amounts of human effort and intellect have been expended in the maintenance and expansion of religion and in understanding the mind of Gods that simple logic say don't exist. This is evidence of how strongly our thoughts are slave to our instincts.

In recent times thoughts about the existence of a supernatural god have begun to change in some parts of the world, but this is not evidence of humans moving beyond their instincts, rather it is because we have found a powerful alternative to satisfy our drives that is incompatible with religious belief. I discuss further below.

Religion being a human invention answers the second part of the question above: why there are so many varieties of religion. It is because there are and have been a large variety of human cultures. To answer the first part, as to why religion is so universal, we can look at how it satisfies our instinctive drives, including those associated with herdism.

The overriding human drive is to survive, as without survival all other drives are for nought. Religion has been constructed to play to this drive. By invoking an afterlife accessible to those who believe in the God(s), adherents are offered the chance of immortality with all that their heart desires, thus guaranteeing everlasting survival. This is a grand prize indeed for those of faith. However, for religion to have so strong a hold over the human mind other needs must also be satisfied in our everyday lives.

For a herd to be cohesive it needs to have a shared purpose and view of the world. Without this shared view, the definition of the group and its necessary distinction from other groups ceases to exist. I contend that this is a primary role of religion in human society. It is a construct to serve as a vehicle for the formulation, distribution and adherence to a shared herd-defining view. Religion is uniquely powerful in doing this as it invokes the supernatural that, by definition, is beyond human control and understanding and so not open to challenge by those who identify as part of the group. If one is a member of a religion they must follow its rules, as they are ordained by a supreme authority. Shared beliefs that do not invoke the supernatural, but are instead overtly based on human thoughts and beliefs, such as environmental action organisations, are more open to internal challenge, leading to weakening of group cohesion.

By invoking the supernatural and identifying the supernatural entity as a particular version of God, it is abundantly clear what must be believed and the rules one must follow to gain group acceptance, while clearly identifying unbelievers that should either be converted to the group's beliefs or shunned in defence of the group. There can be no questioning or dissent, either you do believe in the God or you don't. In religion this is neatly packaged as having faith. To adhere to the religion one is required to take on faith its central tenets, actively rejecting the idea that evidence is required to justify that the beliefs are true. If one does not have faith then one is clearly and definitively not part of the particular herd. This makes religion a perfect vehicle for group definition and to control the behaviour of its adherents.

The strongest religions are ones that bind their members most strongly by demanding the most of them to be accepted, as this more strongly satisfies the herd drive to cooperate and be accepted. They do this in part by defining the religious group most starkly and sharply from others, therefore also providing a strong basis for competing with others. This division is demonstrated by adherence to specific rituals and beliefs and by punishment for non-adherence, be that punishment through social consequences (feeding into our need for acceptance by others, e.g. excommunication) or physical consequences (such as stoning or torture by the Spanish inquisitions). Religions that demand more of their adherents will be stronger and more cohesive than those that allow dissent of thought and action. The strength of commitment is often manifest in the breadth of rules and rituals one has to abide by, the frequency of their practice and the extent to which they require sacrifice. The strongest religions are ones with multiple strong rules, requirements for frequent practice of ritual and where adherence requires individual sacrifice.

This is often expressed as "giving your life to God". This of course has limits. When the demands become too great the self-interest of the individual will override the instinct to belong to the group and most will choose to leave or not participate in the first place. For example, groups with extreme religious practices, that we often label cults, tend to attract relatively small numbers of adherents albeit fanatical ones. Religions that survive the longest have found the point where the demands they impose are as strong as they can be, without causing large numbers of individuals to leave the group through being too out of balance with self-interest.

In the modern world an interesting example of these forces playing out is seen by comparing fundamentalist Christian denominations with the more liberal protestant denominations, such as the Church of England, and the Uniting Church in Australia. The more liberal religions are generally in decline with a dwindling number of aging adherents. In response to the challenge of scientific thinking these Churches have become less comfortable with miracles and the concept of an absolute supernatural God. They have attempted to find a middle ground between these two schools of thought, but in the process eroded one of religion's central reasons for being, a source of unquestionable central authority to provide a strong cohesive force. In the more liberal Churches it is acceptable for members of the Church (not just the Church leaders) to question at least the interpretation of the religious texts and to only perform the Church rituals, such as service of worship attendance or communion, when it is convenient. Allowing questioning and only requiring a nebulous level of commitment diminishes satisfaction of the drive to demonstrate cooperative behaviour. Thus the inclination to be part of that particular group is diminished, leading to its slow dissolution. In contrast, fundamentalist churches demand their members to strongly adhere to the central tenets of the group faith and to regularly and strongly demonstrate their devotion and engagement with the particular deity. This is further reinforced by increased and public demonstrations of devotion tending to lead to increased acceptance and prestige within the group. For example, in more fundamentalist Christian denominations the more publicly you accept God as a real part of your everyday life and pray to him for guidance, the stronger the acceptance of the individual by other group members and the higher their prestige within the group.

Religious motivated terrorism with martyrdom is one of the more extreme manifestations of the power of religion as a cohesive force. In this situation individuals are convinced that it is in their personal best interest to sacrifice their earthly life (and thus their chances of future reproduction) to the interests of their group. Thus the accompanying promise of an afterlife, with access to everything your heart desires, in some cases including multiple sexual partners. If an individual holds these beliefs, committing suicide in the name of the group will simultaneously satisfy their instinctive drives to survive for ever, reproduce through sex (albeit in the afterlife), maximise their group acceptance and prestige while exhorting then to compete against others that are characterised as evil enemies of the group.

It is also therefore not surprising that groups making war have so often done so in the name of religion, as they are both strong manifestations of the drive to satisfy our herd instincts.

It is reasonable to say that today religion is still the strongest and most pervasive force promoting cohesion within groups. According to the Pew Research Center's global study in 2012 (Pew Forum on Religion & Public Life. "The Global Religious Landscape") 84% of the earth's human population were affiliated with a religion in that year. However, at least in the parts of the world where technology and science has had the greatest impact on people's lives, it is also reasonable to say that religious adherence is in decline. These technologically advanced countries tend to have a higher per capita income. International Monetary Fund per capita income data can be combined with the Pew Research Center study figures to study how the development status of a country correlates with religious adherence. Using income data for 2017, for countries in the top 25% of per capita incomes in the world, on average, 35% of the population are not religious. These countries include the northern and western European nations along with the USA, Australia and Japan. For those countries in the bottom 25% per capita income in the world, 16% are not religious. These countries include Central and South American nations, developing African countries, India, Philippines, Vietnam and Cuba. If the communist countries, that actively discourage religious belief, are excluded, the average percentage of the population that is not religious for this group drops to 9%. Thus there is a stark difference in religious affiliation between the developed, wealthier countries and the developing poorer countries. I believe this is the result of a shift in the source of drive satisfaction for individuals in high per capita income countries.

From a herdism perspective it is interesting that communist doctrine seeks to so strongly suppress religious belief. Carl Marx, the father of communism saw religion as the "opiate of the people", as a way the authorities could keep the population compliant and accepting of an inherently unfair system. That is, that the cooperative behaviour manifest in religious adherence was used by the society's small controlling classes to balance their selfish behaviour.

Herdism would say that religion is the enemy of communism, as it is an alternative way that people can satisfy their herd instincts. For true communism to function it requires cooperative behaviour to strongly dominate in the governed population. This is not the optimal way to satisfy our instincts. That requires a balance with selfish behaviour. To counter loss of satisfaction of the drive to be selfish, communism seeks to strengthen satisfaction of the need for acceptance and cohesion through requiring strong adherence to communist doctrine to the exclusion of all others, especially religion with its strong satisfaction of those same needs. Making communist belief the only available way these instincts can be satisfied is a powerful way of manipulating the population to see communism as the essential centre of the lives. Strong external threat to the herd from the corrupt capitalist west was also used to reinforce the need for the protection of the communist state, along with threat to a dissenting individual's survival through incarceration and death, to suppress their desire for instinct satisfaction through other means.

In communist countries religion has been actively suppressed to prevent the people having divided loyalty between the state and the church. But why is religion also disappearing in other parts of the world?

In developed countries technology is increasingly providing lower effort access to resources for the individual. By this I mean that technology is decreasing the physical and mental effort required to get what you want and allow you to get more of it. You no longer have to be in a particularly privileged position in society or work very hard, to have access to shelter, entertainment and food produced cheaply and in abundance. With the advent of cars, television, smartphones and the Internet most people in these societies don't have to walk anywhere, or remember much or think about much or work very hard to gain the resources to prosper. The agricultural revolution led by scientific understanding has made access to abundant food far easier for most of the population. Thus the application of science and technology has by and large led to a large net increase in resources available to the individual (i.e. an increase in resources gained with a decrease in the resources used to get them) with an accompanying increase in their security of survival. This is recognised, either consciously or subconsciously, by individuals who have benefited and thus they tend to associate adherence to scientific beliefs with satisfaction of the drive to increase their net resources and survival. The demonstrable benefits of science to enhance survival are thus replacing the less tangible benefit of possible admission to an afterlife. In contrast, in countries where the benefits of science and technology are not felt by most of the population, religious belief still dominates.

But why do humans engage in scientific endeavour? If we are so controlled by our instincts, why do we spend resources on what appears to be the opposite of instinctive behaviour, that is, the pursuit of rational objective thought and evidence-based conclusions? The answer is that the pursuit of science is just as much a behaviour that satisfies our instinctive drives as, for example, not jumping off a cliff. A primary aim of science and technology is to understand our world and with that understanding be able to predict and control it to our benefit. Thus these endeavours satisfy the drive to survive. The more successful we are in using science and technology to improve our situation, the stronger the drive satisfaction will be. This explains the rise of science and technology as a social force over the last century accompanied by a decline in religion. The industrial revolution was the beginning of a tipping point where the accumulated knowledge of science became sufficient for the survival benefits to be felt by a significant portion of the population. Before this time science and technology were mainly to the benefit of small scholar classes and in the waging of war. With the ability to use machines to mass produce items and ever more complicated tools, along with the acceleration in medicine and understanding of disease and food production, science and technology started to be of benefit to all. This began the march to replace faith in an afterlife with belief in the survival benefits that science can provide. Rather than science being an example of human activity that only uses the "rational" mind, it is, like everything else humans do, a result of our drive to satisfy our instincts.

In countries where the benefits of technology are not felt by most of the people, in the past or today, it is religion that tends to dominate. The satisfaction of drives is maximised by using religion to satisfy our herd and survival instincts, as there is little opportunity for most individuals to otherwise improve their material and survival position in these societies. However, as the power of science and technology increases, the balance shifts, where satisfaction of the drive to survive and have a net resource gain through science outweighs drive satisfaction through religion.

Strong acceptance of the tenets of scientific thought leaves adherents with a dilemma, for in accepting these tenets they must abandon one of the strongest satisfiers of their herd instincts, religious belief in a supernatural being with absolute authority. This does not mean that with the adoption of a belief in science the need to satisfy our herd instincts has decreased, just that we can no longer see religious belief, with its absolute requirement to have unquestioning faith, as a viable way to satisfy those needs.

Humans have introduced a number of new concepts in an attempt to resolve this conflict between the satisfaction of different drives. One attempt has been to blend scientific thought with religious belief, leading to such statements as "science can answer how but only God can answer why", or viewing such things as creation by God and miracles of the bible not as literal accounts but allegorical stories, designed to help us better understand the mind of God. These attempts must necessarily lead to the diminution of faith, as they draw boundaries around what aspects of the religious beliefs must be accepted on faith and which aspects can be questioned or dismissed. Once faith becomes less than absolute it is no longer faith, but rather selective acceptance based upon preference.

The opposite approach is also being trialled, where it is promulgated by religious leaders that to adhere to a religion a strong rejection of scientific thought is required. Religious practice in parts of the USA is a case in point, where the creationist movement and denial of Darwinian evolution is a prime example of this phenomenon. This is likely to be a stopgap measure at best, as science and technology is constantly increasing its power and influence over the lives of people, whereas the tools open to those wanting to shore up religious dogma are by and large static.

Another attempt that has had some success is to emphasise the aspects of religious practice that most strongly satisfy the herd instinct drives, so they can compete more strongly against the drive for survival and net resource gain though science. Thus the increasing presence and popularity of the evangelical churches that demand complete immersion of the individual in the religion, with them giving their lives over to God. I suspect it is also a driving force in the rise of the fundamentalist Islamic religious groups, who reject all but their sect's version of the teachings of Allah.

Despite these efforts, a large and increasing number of people living in technologically advanced nations have largely rejected religion and a belief in a supernatural being. So how do they now satisfy their drive for group acceptance and identity? Where can individuals now look for a source of what they should believe and how they should behave to be part of their herd? One place people have looked is the mass media. It provides an avenue where the same information, ideas, opinions and explicit or implicit instructions on how one should behave can be simultaneously communicated to huge numbers of people. This results in a large proportion of the other people with which an individual has daily contact having the same information provided by the mass media. If humans see behaviour and ideas that agree with those previously experienced, the behaviour and ideas tend to be reinforced. Individuals following instruction provided by the mass media will feel part of a larger group by knowing that they share experiences, knowledge and opinions with those they come into contact with.

Chapter 12

Politics

Is there a "best" political system?

Living in herds requires authorities that provide rules by which herd members must abide to be accepted. This is what political system and government is. It, along with religion, has provided a shared view of acceptable and non-acceptable behaviour along with enforcement measures such as the police force that function to maintain a balance of selfish and cooperative behaviour in the society. For social animals, some sort of recognised leadership structure is inevitable, however the form of that structure will be variable. But how do we judge a "good" from a "bad" political system and indeed if there is a "best" system?

The answer to this depends upon your definition of "best". A political system will be most sustainable if it most strongly satisfies the instinctive drives of the people it governs. For herd instincts this includes maintaining a balance between cooperative and selfish behaviours, while increasing individuals' access to resources and chances of survival.

In politics the language often used to characterise one's beliefs is right versus left wing. Right wing politics tends to emphasise the individual more, where it is believed that the optimal point for a society is one where the individual is allowed to be selfish within controlled limits, as that will generate the most wealth and stability for the society overall. Left wing politics tends to emphasise the wider society more, where an optimal outcome occurs when richer individuals are required to contribute more towards the welfare of others and where power is more evenly shared. In herdism terms this translates to a balance point being further towards selfish behaviour for those with right wing political leanings versus cooperative behaviour for those with left wing political leanings. Simplistically, right wing can thus be replaced with being more selfish and left wing with being more cooperative. However, before those with left wing political views jump to claim the moral high ground, it should be remembered that in herdism both selfish and cooperative behaviours are useful, valid and necessary for optimal survival. Thus left and right wing political beliefs are two sides of the same coin. Both have merit and will satisfy our instincts best when both are present and in balance.

Herdism thus suggests that systems between moderate socialism and moderate capitalism should be most successful in keeping the people satisfied, with resultant strong and sustainable group cohesion. Systems that seek to impose excessive cooperation should be unsustainable, as should systems that allow excessively selfish behaviour. Communist doctrine is an example of a system that had as its goal a society where cooperative behaviours strongly dominate selfish behaviours. The experience of the European eastern bloc shows us that an excess of cooperative behaviour cannot be sustained firstly within the system (leading to the rise of a governing elite that demonstrated selfish behaviours) and ultimately leading to the collapse of the system.

China is an interesting case that is currently evolving. That system appears to be rebalancing the mix of condoned cooperative and selfish behaviours by adopting elements of individual free enterprise within a nominal system that espouses cooperation over personal reward.

Capitalist systems, if taken in their pure form, tend to an imbalance towards selfish behaviour, where the aim is to exploit the resources of others for personal gain. If this imbalance gets to the point where the culture does not sufficiently value herd cohesion, the society will be labelled as "unfair" by large sections of the people and will either start to splinter and disintegrate into smaller insurgent, ethnic or class groups or revolution will occur.

Autocracies are another example of a political system that can result in excessively selfish behaviour. Examples from history of these being unsustainable when the behaviour became too extreme are the French, Russian and Chinese revolutions. It is perhaps predictable from herdism that in all these cases the system that replaced the autocracy was one that strongly emphasised cooperative behaviour. The extreme reaction to the excessive selfishness of the previous regime led to an over emphasis of cooperative behaviour in the new regimes, that was also out of balance to best satisfy the herd instincts of the people. The new French revolutionary government quite quickly reintroduced some selfish behaviour characterised by revenge against old enemies and a new elite class forming, however where the people still had more influence than previously. It was a similar situation in Russia and China, however these regimes imposed cooperative behaviour systems such as communes upon their people for longer than occurred in France.

It we accept the premise that a political system is most sustainable if it continues to meet the instinctive drives of the people it governs, then it follows that in general democratic systems should be more sustainable in the long term than autocratic systems, as democratic systems have in-built mechanisms to prevent large imbalances persisting.

However, there then comes the question of what is "best" for humanity? From the discussion above it is somewhat self-evident that a political system where the people have the power to shape it to meet their instinctive drives will be popular and sustainable. However, what is also apparent from our human experience is that there are limits to the effectiveness of meeting our instinctive drives as a mechanism for ensuring our individual and humanity's and thus our genes', optimum survival.

When abundant high calorie food is available and physical effort can be replaced by burning fossil fuels, a large number of us cannot seem to stop eating ourselves to an early death. When there is abundant evidence of the damage burning those fossil fuels will do to our environment we fail to stop, as to do so would make life harder in the present. We are thus trading the long-term survival of our genes for the short-term pleasure of satisfying our instinctive drives.

As a species we care much more about what might happen now and in the near future than we do about longer timescales. I think this is a consequence of the evolutionary process. Preoccupation with the present arises from the instinct to survive in a dangerous world. If we do not survive imminent threats we have no further ability to spread our genes. After we have had children, the carriers of our genes, we also care about their ability to survive and successfully reproduce. Thus the important time horizon to us, our horizon of care, tends to be our own lifetime and up to when our children have successfully procreated. When our current brain structure evolved humans rarely lived much past the birth of their grandchildren, so there was no reason for our brains to evolve the capacity to care beyond that time horizon. Thus we instinctively tend to care about our remaining lifespan and perhaps that of our children, but no further. This may be one reason why people in their late teens and early twenties seem to more actively care about the future of their world than their parents. When you are born your time horizon of care is set and the year will not change as you age. Middle to late teens of child bearing age start to instinctively care about the chances of survival of their future children, but since they are earlier in the cycle than their parents, have a longer time period over which they care. As they age, their individual horizon doesn't move, so the time period they care about shrinks. Politics is generally dominated by older individuals, so it is perhaps not very surprising that politicians have difficulty dealing with issues that will only occur in the future.

As we have used our brains to shape the world to our advantage over the timescale we care about, we have developed the power to impact much longer timescales. The reality is our actions will now have long-term impacts, but we are not equipped to care about what they are, so we inevitably revert to gaining emotional rewards by satisfying our instinctive shorter-term needs.

Another reality is that although we are driven by our instincts, we have also developed the capacity to recognise and understand that this is the case. Understanding gives us the ability to step outside our instinctive urges and look at them critically to see if they are actually in our best interest. If we can maintain and act on this critical evaluation, we can modify our behaviour to respond in ways that are truly best for the survival of our genes. In this way we can start to move beyond our immediate instinctive urges with their inherent limitations.

This is where judgement of the "best" political system becomes more complicated. If the role of government is to satisfy the needs of most of its people most of the time, then systems that can successfully maintain a balance of cooperative and selfish behaviours, or even more powerfully simultaneously satisfy the drives to cooperate, compete and increase individual survival, prestige and resources, could be judged as the best systems. However, as we have discussed, the satisfaction of people's instinctive needs is not necessarily in the best interests of humanity beyond their horizon of care. Our reasoning brains give us the ability to be aware of and consider these longer-term needs. Should government take a greater role in responding to the longer-term needs of humanity, even though the responses in some instances may be to the detriment of our short-term desires? In other words, should government seek to act as a collective human brain that steps outside our instinctive responses, to try to optimise the survival of the herd it governs beyond their instinctive horizon of care? This happens to some extent today, with agreements such as the Kyoto and Paris Accords, but their effectiveness is limited.

Democratic systems such as we have today may be optimal for responding to the instinctive needs of their constituents; as to stay in power a government must do so. However, this is likely to mean they will be poor at being able to act in ways that enhance survival beyond the horizon of care, particularly if those actions mean a poorer satisfaction of individuals' instinctive needs within their horizon. This is evident in the actions of these governments. The response to human induced climate change is an obvious case in point, where wholesale changes to how those societies behave have not and will not be made until the effects enter our horizon of care. It is therefore interesting to note that the emerging world leader in addressing human induced climate change is China.

The Chinese system of government allows it to maintain power even though it might not always be responding to the short-term needs of its people. China is also in the process of rebalancing the officially condoned behaviours towards individual satisfaction, where in the past cooperative behaviour was over-emphasised to optimally satisfy its people's instinctive needs. Simultaneously, a large number of Chinese are increasing their personal wealth. So at a time when more individuals in China are feeling an increase in their personal satisfaction, they are perhaps more accepting of actions that may not benefit them in the short term. This, in combination with the lesser ability of the population to remove the government, the resources the government has at its disposal and the acute nature of some current environmental issues in China today, gives it a prime opportunity to successfully create positive changes that affect humanity beyond our horizon of care.

Of course, there are also all the dangers inherent in this situation. The enhanced outcomes for humanity depend upon the actions of a few, who are subject to the same instinctive drives as all of humanity. Thus using their power to enhance the propagation of their genes though excessively selfish behaviour, to the detriment of the herd they lead. This, typically termed corruption, is an ever-present danger in situations where individuals have excessive personal power. If this occurs unchecked, the balance between cooperative and selfish behaviour in government action is destroyed.

The key is to be able to maintain a balance of cooperative and selfish behaviour within a government system while encouraging it to have a long-term vision. The ability to implement a longer-term vision is very limited in current democratic systems, where governments tend to focus on their prospects of re-election rather than laws that would change the mid to long-term future of the people they govern. This is not the fault of the politicians, but rather a consequence of the system in which they work.

I think there are measures that could be taken to encourage a sustainable government with a longer-term view. The system should ensure that decisions are taken by a diverse group of individuals, rather than the current system where most politicians follow the party line dictated by a few. It should create a situation where that group does not need to maintain its power by satisfying the short-term needs of the people it governs to the detriment of their longer-term survival.

Via the constitution of the country the governing body should be explicitly charged with the responsibility of considering the next fifty years when drafting legislation. This is still within the horizon of care of a large portion of the people being represented, but long enough to prevent an exclusive short-term view. To ensure that this responsibility is implemented, every piece of legislation would have to include the projected effects of it over the fifty-year period. If these were not judged to be acceptable during consideration of the bill, the legislation could not be passed as it would be unconstitutional.

A possible model for a governing body that is sustainable and has the ability to consider the longer-term is one consisting of a group of elected individuals, that can be members of a traditional party within government, but where it is mandated that legislation is passed via secret ballot and that no individual is required to vote along their party line. In this way, the drive to be part of a group can be satisfied for the politicians, but not to the preclusion of their individual conscience. Parties must therefore work harder to build internal consensus and thus be less dominated by the beliefs of powerful individuals within the party, in other words, to function and have power as a group they must be cooperative. To guard against corrupt behaviour such as bribery to vote a particular way, an independent body would be established that views the votes and oversees behaviour, where the votes are published with some delay, so constituents can still assess the behaviour of their elected representative.

A likely consequence of removing the requirement to vote along party lines is that it will be more difficult to pass legislation, as more individuals will need to be convinced of the merits of the laws. To counter this and create a balance of cooperative and selfish behaviour in government, a system that enhances the power of individuals that choose to cooperate with others in the parliament can be created. In an exemplar system vote points would be awarded to individuals as a reward for cooperation in allowing legislation that they can accept to be passed. That is, politicians that voted for legislation that was passed are awarded points while those who voted against the legislation are not. There would be no points allocated for legislation that did not pass. Note that the points would be allocated via automated systems such that the ballots remained secret. When enough points have been accumulated by an individual, they are awarded an extra vote to be used on any future issue they wish. Thus, in areas an individual or party feels passionate about, they can increase their personal power by cooperating with others in areas where they either agree or can live with the outcome.

To give government the opportunity to be less concerned about the immediate satisfaction of their constituent's needs and more focused on optimisation in the longer term, it would be important that the group had an appropriate time window for action, where individuals had perhaps a 5 to 10 year term, with more frequent rolling regular local elections that work through the group over time, allowing some constant renewal on a background of longer term stability.

In such a system, the secret mandatory conscience vote means the power of any party leader or faction is diminished, as they can only act as a guiding hand to help individuals through issues, rather than as a sole source and enforcer of particular doctrine. If pressure is applied to individuals to vote a particular way, the legislated nature of the conscience vote means bullying politicians would be open to prosecution.

Such a government should have an improved capacity to implement longer-term agendas, while guarding against the danger of excessive power allowing selfish behaviour to become out of balance with cooperative behaviour, both within the governing body and in how they govern. It should also strongly satisfy the instinctive needs of the politicians, allowing them to be part of a group (their declared party), to act cooperatively within their party and with others, to gain personal power and prestige and to compete with the other parties and within their own party by using their extra votes to win when they feel strongly about an issue. The longer terms for individuals (although not for the party group as a whole) would also tend to give personal stability and, assuming they are well paid, increased personal wealth. This should help to attract highly capable people to participate.

Chapter 13

Climate Change

Why is engagement with the issue of human-induced climate change so difficult and can it be increased?

A great preponderance of scientific evidence indicates that human activity has induced a warming of the earth that, if left unchecked, will have dire consequences for humanity and other life. It is hard to imagine an issue of greater scale or importance to humanity, but for decades a large proportion of the population has failed to become fully engaged or act decisively to address it.

Herdism theory speaks to why this is so and suggests ways to increase engagement. Our herd instincts drive us to cooperate, compete and maintain a balance between the two. If asked to only cooperate or only compete we feel out of balance, with only one drive being satisfied. This is usually accompanied by a sense of unfairness, as we instinctively equate fairness with a balance between our self-interest and the interests of others.

Combating climate change has been framed almost exclusively as a cooperative venture. The world must work together to address it. There have been multiple summits, accords and agreements on emission targets and pronouncements of the dire consequences of not meeting them, but little talk of the need or ability to embrace climate change as an opportunity, through which groups or countries can compete and win. The only real element of competition so far has been between so called climate change deniers and climate change activists. As we know, competing is a necessary part of human behaviour, so it is not surprising that this divide exists, but it is not one that is useful in addressing the pressing issue of global warming. This type of competition serves to entrench already polarised positions, working against the advancement of both sides' agenda.

Groups such as Extinction Rebellion seek to spur action on climate change, but by strongly competing with those who either wish to deny or ignore climate change, they encourage the opposite behaviour to that they seek. By being a clearly identifiable enemy of climate change inaction, Extinction Rebellion encourage a stronger reaction in climate change deniers, as through strong rejection of the Extinction Rebellion message they can satisfy their drives to compete and cooperate. The more intense the fight the stronger the drive satisfaction. Deniers obtain stronger emotional rewards by working against climate change than they would if groups such as Extinction Rebellion did not exist.

Equally, the broad aims of climate change deniers, those of optimising current and short-term economic prosperity, are frustrated by placing themselves in opposition to a large fraction of the community that are concerned about the issue. Their plans, such as opening new coal mines or oil fields, are frustrated by the competition they face from climate change protesters. The more strongly they push their prosperity agenda, the stronger the instinctive drives of those that oppose them will be satisfied through protestation.

It is instructive that the divide between climate change deniers and believers tends to be along political lines, where those with right wing political leanings tend to deny or ignore climate change and those with left wing political leanings tend to be engaged. According to herdism theory, this divide is associated with where an individual sees the optimum balance point between cooperative and competitive behaviour. Those with more right wing views tend to see the balance point that works best for them being tipped towards competitive behaviour, where those with left wing views see it tipped towards cooperative behaviour. That the climate change debate has so far been framed in cooperative terms is consistent with the political divide between deniers and believers.

The attitude of the USA in the debate is also consistent with this theory. In earlier times, when President Obama, a left-wing leaning politician, was leading the USA, they were at least politically engaged in the debate, even if the President found it difficult to bring all the people along with him. With the election of President Trump, a firmly right-wing leaning politician, the leadership has tried to completely disengage from the debate and any associated required actions. The culture of the USA is intrinsically competitive and so it was always going to be a struggle to bring the country to believe in what has been framed as a purely cooperative endeavour. They would instinctively and culturally see the global approach to climate change as grossly out of balance behaviour and thus unfair on them, with the rest of the world telling them what to do. Seen in this light it is hardly surprising that a president that strongly reflects this sense of unfairness was chosen by the people.

What herdism theory tells us is that the behaviour of people is strongly driven by their herd instincts. To engage individuals in the fight against climate change more fully it must more strongly satisfy those instincts. What has been lacking to date in the way the fight against climate change has been framed is a balance between cooperative and competitive elements. For a large number of individuals it is seen as purely cooperative, thus out of balance and unfair that they have to change to address it. Hence the feeling of being put upon by government or other countries seeking to curtail their freedom to behave as they wish and the rise of competition between climate change activists and deniers.

The fight against climate change is an example of how different behaviours can be adopted to satisfy our instincts in a more positive way for humanity and the planet. We are driven to compete and cooperate, but within the current climate change movement there is no strong competitive element to help satisfy that instinct. To find this element and thus experience a stronger feeling of fairness, we are driven towards opposing climate change action or fighting those that oppose it.

This situation can be changed by emphasising the opportunities to compete and win through addressing climate change. There is after all a real and huge opportunity here. Successfully addressing climate change requires a planetary overhaul of the energy production and consumption technologies and systems we use within a couple of decades. What bigger market prize could there be? A huge potential market with massive growth over a short timescale. The companies and countries that are successful in producing these technologies and systems first, have the chance to dominate the planet in the coming decades, both economically and in prestige. This turns the current lose-lose competitive situation where climate activists and climate deniers fight for their ideology, to a win-win situation, where addressing climate change results in enhanced prosperity and prestige for those who achieve it. Under this paradigm it is not necessary to believe that climate change is real to profit from it, just that enough other people in the world believe it to create a market.

An example of what can be achieved in a short period of time for what may seem an abstract goal is the space race of the 1960's. This was intensely competitive between the USSR and the USA and required nationwide cooperation and focus to make it happen. It had all the elements to strongly satisfy our instincts. As well as intense cooperation and competition a huge amount of prestige was and still is associated with putting man on the moon, hence the efforts of India and China to do so now and the USA renewed interest in repeating their past glories in this endeavour. This is despite there being few if any direct material benefits of achieving the goal. The material benefits were largely indirect in spurring development of new civilian and military technologies. The primary benefit was prestige in winning the race.

The prize for successfully addressing climate change is at least an order of magnitude larger than winning the space race, in all the ways that matter to humans. It will confer huge amounts of money and prestige upon the winners, while capturing the imagination of the population, requiring them to strongly cooperate within their herd to win the prize. The competitive element of the climate change effort therefore needs to be shifted away from deniers competing with believers, to competition between groups and countries to develop the technologies and infrastructure to dominate the world in the post-fossil-fuel era. This change will advance the agendas of both sides, as economic prosperity can be increased by acting to address climate change. To do this a reframing of the debate is required. Rather than summits being held to try to get countries to cooperate, studies need to be done to show the economic and social opportunities addressing climate change represents. Countries like Japan, South Korea and China have already realised this and are on the journey to win the prize. Evidence of this is their progress towards a hydrogen-based economy with large government sponsored programs on such things as battery and fuel cell technology development and hydrogen distribution infrastructure. The threat to the superiority of other nations not embracing this challenge needs to be emphasised if their governments and populations are to be successfully engaged in the fight.

To those with left-wing political leanings, pursuing this course may seem like a lost opportunity to get the world to finally cooperate on a global scale. Instead, humanity is once again giving into the greed and avarice that created the issue in the first place. What the evidence tells us is that cooperation alone can never be effective in the long term, as our brains are simply not wired that way. What is most effective is to allow us to cooperate and compete simultaneously to improve our material position and our prestige. This is the way to encourage change.

Chapter 14

Life's Purpose

Why are we here and what is our purpose?

Any self-respecting book considering the big questions in life should include what is often thought of as the biggest question for humans: why are we here and what is our purpose? In my view the Darwinian theory of evolution via natural selection provides a clear and sufficient answer, which may not be particularly satisfying to many, but is nevertheless true.

We are here because our parents survived and gave birth to us, as did their parents before them etcetera, in an unbroken chain to the earliest living organism on earth (or at least the earliest organism that resulted in hominids, if life arose spontaneously more than once). So in pure Darwinian terms, our sole purpose in life is to produce new vehicles for our genes, that is, have children. If that were not the purpose of a life-form, that life-form would cease to exist when the current generation died. To be here, that is to exist, our primary purpose must be to reproduce.

However, because we live in a world where we compete for resources, we not only need to have the mechanisms and will to reproduce, but also the ability for ourselves and our offspring to survive threats. This imperative explains the presence of the other instinctive drives that are the subject of this book. These additional instincts provide what I think of as secondary or supporting purpose for our life, that is, things we are driven to do to support our primary purpose of reproduction. Thus, people find purpose in such things as being a good neighbour or friend, volunteering their time in the service of others, becoming a top athlete, being the best parent they can be or gathering as much money as they can for as little effort as possible. We find purpose in such things as they satisfy our herd instincts to compete and cooperate, nurture and gain acceptance of the groups to which we belong and gain extra resources and prestige for ourselves. Even if individuals do not have the opportunity to, or choose not to reproduce, satisfying our other instinctive drives can still provide a satisfying and fulfilling life with purpose. Also of course there is a large amount of diversity among humans, so while some people feel strongly driven to have children others do not. There is sufficient breadth in our instinctive drives that there are many ways to feel fulfilled.

To some this analysis may appear harsh, ignoring such things as our love of music and art, the love for our children, partners, families and friends and the deep grief that we can feel with loss. I do not believe this to be so. These things are real and driven by strong emotions that we feel very deeply. Seeking to understand the source of these emotions does not detract from those feelings or invalidate them. Understanding why we feel the way we do can enhance the emotions and richness of life. What must be abandoned if we are to move forward is the thought that these things are somehow magical and beyond understanding, as this belief leaves us powerless to exert control over them if we wish to do so.

As posed in the last chapter, is satisfying these instinctive drives still the best way to survive in a world where our technology has drastically increased our power to transform the environment upon which we rely? Can we use our rational mind to recognise that we do not always act in the long-term best interest of our genes and so be able to behave in ways not driven by short-term emotional reward and punishment? In other words, can we use the accumulated wisdom of the human species to move beyond our evolved responses, to live in a way that is ultimately more sustainable?

Our technological power to consume the planet's resources is increasing at an exponential rate and is far outstripping the ability of natural selection to adapt our brain structures appropriately. Either we are heading for a catastrophic adjustment when the finite resources run out, we annihilate each other as rival herds, or we learn to change our behaviour to place long-term sustainable survival ahead of the short-term emotional satisfaction.

Since our rational minds are the only tool we have to counter our instincts, if we are to move beyond behaviour driven by instinctive urges we must increase the power that our rational thoughts have over our behaviour. This is where I think an increased understanding of what motivates our behaviour can help. By using rational thought to intercede between emotional response and action, we have a chance to change what we do. To do this we each need to recognise in real time the process our mind is going through from stimulus, to emotional response and then action.

Consciously understanding why we feel the way we do in response to a stimulus can be a circuit breaker, giving our rational thoughts the chance to intervene in our behaviour choice, so we don't just act because "we feel like doing it". Rather, we act because we have rationally decided that the action is the best way to achieve our aspirations.

Chapter 15

Instinct and Free Will

A difficulty many people have with the concept that they are driven by instinct is that it doesn't feel like that in everyday life. Unless we are physically constrained, including constraints like not having enough money to buy food, we can and do choose how we behave and what we do every minute of every day. If I can choose what I want to do, how can I be a slave to my instincts? In fact, freedom to choose and being driven by instincts are quite compatible.

The question is not whether or not we have freedom of choice, unless prevented by our circumstances we can do as we please. Even if we feel constrained in our choices, such as someone living under a repressive regime not feeling free to publicly speak their mind, they can still choose whether or not to speak out, with the choice being informed by their wish to be true to what they believe versus fear of retribution. They still make a choice, albeit perhaps a different one to that made if living in a society where freedom of speech is allowed.

The real question revolves around the source of our will. Another word for will is desire. What we want to do and what we desire to do are just two different words for the same thing. Using the word desire however, more openly associates it with satisfying our emotions. These emotions are not generated by thought. A thought is neutral unless given emotional context. For example, the thought of making a sandwich is neutral in the sense it is not associated with any will to do so, the will arises from feeling hungry. Similarly, the thought of killing someone is neutral, with the will to do so being dictated by emotions such as fear, revenge, disgust, greed etc.

Our will does not arise from what we think, it comes from what we feel. It is the source of those emotions that is at question when considering whether or not we have free will. Emotion is nature's way of making us act upon our instinctive drives; thus, our will is generated by our instincts. This does not remove freedom of choice, so is quite compatible with our everyday experience of choosing our actions, what it does do is channel our actions so that we seek to gain emotional reward and avoid emotional pain.

To take the example above, even though I am hungry I still have a choice of whether or not to make a sandwich. My choice may be to not make one if I feel tired or lazy, rather I get food delivered, or that I know I will feel good if I lose weight, so accept that overall the emotional pay-off will be greater if I have a piece of fruit instead. The choices still exist, but the will to act comes from how the action makes me feel.

The logic that underpins instinct being the source of our actions is fairly simple and compelling. It goes like this.

For instincts to be present and widespread in a population, be it other animal or human, they must have been conserved in the DNA coding transferred between generations, such that successive generations have a higher proportion of individuals with this coding.

For the DNA coding corresponding to an instinct to be preserved and widespread in a population, the individuals that possess that coding need to have a greater chance of survival and reproduction than other individuals. This is exactly analogous to DNA coding conferring increased strength or intellectual ability to enhance survival and procreation.

For an instinct to lead to enhanced survival and reproduction it must be expressed as action. If no action is taken as the result of possessing an instinct, it is moot and will have no impact on the life of the organism possessing it.

The mechanism of evolution thus requires a way of translating instinct to action. Emotion is this vehicle. It is our reason for action. We do not act because of what we think, we act because of the way those actions make us feel. Thoughts can dictate how we act but emotions dictate if we act.

Emotion is not generated by thought. Thoughts are emotionally neutral; they are an interpretation of the world and often associated with emotions, but do not generate them. The only abstract output of our brain, based upon the inputs we receive, are thoughts and emotions. If thought is neutral, that only leaves emotion as the thing that can drive action, based on the inputs received.

Since action is only driven by emotion and emotion is only driven by instinct, it follows that all our actions must be driven by instinct. I find this a very powerful and somewhat disturbing conclusion, but one that is inescapable. Instead of the oft quoted contention of Descartes "I think therefore I am" a more powerful truth is perhaps "I feel therefore I act", with the accompanying fact that my instincts are generating those feelings.

I find this personally disturbing. By accepting my actions are instinctive I don't feel in control of my life, but I suspect the uncomfortable feeling is a trick of my instincts. Manipulation of action is much more effective if the manipulated is unaware. The fact that I exist is, to a large extent, a result of my ancestors and I acting upon the instincts coded into our DNA, keeping us safe and driving us to procreate. That we did so mean our actions were effectively manipulated by our instincts. So those that have survived are those coded to be unaware of being manipulated, thus an uncomfortable feeling being associated with attempting to become aware of the manipulation. By acknowledging and living with this discomfort I can continue to be aware of the forces driving me and more cognisant of the choices that I have and can act upon.

That instincts drive our actions is a central truth that needs to be acknowledged if we are to continue to advance as a species. Without this recognition we will continue to be powerless to prevent our own decimation. Manifest technological prowess and organizational sophistication encourage us to believe we are in control of our instincts and thus above other animals. The amount of material resources and intellectual effort expended on such things as war, religion, fashion and sport show us this is not the case. Looked at objectively, these activities are a huge waste of the world's finite resources, nevertheless our lives are often dominated by them.

It is foolhardy to think we can just ignore our instincts. They are deeply rooted in our brain structures and will take many generations of living under altered environmental stresses to change that basic structure via adaption. There is hope however. Even though instincts continue to drive us, we do have the opportunity to choose how to satisfy them. We all make these choices today, using our memories to help choose behaviour that will best satisfy our instincts. By being aware we are doing this we can further inform those choices. This is the subject of the next chapter.

Chapter 16

Where to From Here?

This book and many others show that, at least intellectually, we can understand that our behaviour is driven by gaining emotional rewards and avoiding emotional punishment by satisfying our instincts. It is clear that satisfying those instincts has guided us to become the dominant life-form on earth, if not in number, then certainly in ability to modify the earth to our liking.

The difficulty is that we have become too good at satisfying those instincts. Through the ability to cooperate, communicate and build and manipulate tools we have developed the power to effect outcomes on a much larger scale than was possible when our species evolved. Rather than an individual only being able to injure or kill one other person at a time, now an individual can kill millions at one stroke through their use of thermonuclear weapons. Similarly, rather than an individual only being able to clear their local area of vegetation or contaminate a local water hole, humanity can now combine to modify the climate of the entire planet for decades if not hundreds of years to come. We are mal-adapted to the situation in which we find ourselves. Rather than our instinctive drives working to promulgate our genes, their satisfaction can lead to species wide decimation or destruction.

I don't think that it is possible to just ignore our instinctive drives to solve the problem. Analysis of how instincts act upon us and our history show that this is too hard for humans to achieve at any significant scale.

Instead, I think a way out of this dilemma is to modify how we choose to satisfy those drives. If more of us more fully understand what is driving our behaviour and the effect our current actions are having, we can choose better ways to satisfy our instincts.

Some things are making this change easier to achieve than in the past. As discussed in earlier chapters, humans overall are increasing their acceptance of science and technology as they experience more fully how it can satisfy their instinctive drive for an easier and more secure life. Perhaps this increased acceptance can be used to increase awareness of the role instincts play in driving our behaviour? It could also increase the trust individuals put in the predictions of science on things that may not be evident within our horizon of care.

For example, when an individual wants to deny that climate change exists because it conflicts with their instinctive drive to maximise their net resource gain (though using cheap fossil fuels to do all the work), they can recognise this is happening. That recognition can change the thought process from "defend myself by denying climate change" to "defend myself by resisting my natural urge to deny climate change and instead consider my optimal future survival". The basic instinctive motivation to defend remains, but the outcome for the planet can be very different.

As well as on an individual level, this change can be built into our political institutions. As suggested in this book, the systems can be modified so that politicians still satisfy their instinctive drives by participating in the political process, but are specifically charged with finding ways of satisfying the drives of their constituents in ways that conflict less with the ultimate health and survival of the human species. This changes the messages given by the source of authority to the herd. As individuals think beyond their immediate instinctive responses, the chance that these new messages will be accepted is increased. These two factors can work together to create positive change.

This book is an attempt to contribute to individuals having the ability to think beyond their immediate instinctive urges, by better understanding their motivations. Much more work is required, but the discussion should continue.

To better understand and accept the true consequences of our actions, trust in the objectivity of the scientific process needs to be increased. This will be assisted by continuing to use technology to improve the lives of a greater portion of the human species. Having broad-based bodies sponsor the pursuit of new scientific knowledge to increase the objectivity of conclusions could also assist in gaining wider acceptance. Spreading the benefits of technology should happen naturally, as profit-driven development is rolled out to the developing world, with programs like the Bill and Melinda Gates Foundation accelerating the process. Increasing the independence of scientific research can be aided by, for example, expanding the research programs sponsored by bodies such as the United Nations and directing them to study the effects of current human behaviour on the long-term survival of the human species. This research should not only consider the effect of human actions, but also their motivation. If an explicit coupling is made from instinct to emotion, to action, to effect, the new knowledge can be seen in the context of why we currently act the way we do and potentially help to find other ways to satisfy the same instincts that have a better outcome for humanity.

A disadvantage of having large broad-based bodies is that they are counter to our instinct to divide and compete. To accommodate these instincts an alternative approach would be to set up and fund a number of smaller bodies charged with researching the same issue and allow them to compete to find the best solutions, with the winner receiving recognition and further funding. These bodies could still be multinational and multiracial, making it more likely that their conclusions are widely accepted, but placed in competition with other such bodies. Alternatively, they could be nationally based and thus satisfy the instinct to compete as national groups, which historically has been a very strong incentive to act.

In addressing climate change for example, a race to win the prestige and economic dominance that will come with successfully developing the technologies and systems necessary to replace fossil fuels can be encouraged to develop naturally. This can be kick-started through studies showing the potential market size and growth for developed solutions, so that governments and corporations can appreciate the size of the prize that awaits the winners, whether or not they personally believe in climate change. This changes the perception from one of economic burden and threat to economic opportunity. It fully engages our competitive and cooperative natures. It doesn't matter if we believe the threat of climate change is real; as long as others do we can sell our solutions, increase our prestige and repel the threat of other groups getting there first. If climate change is real, we win by reducing its causes, if it is not real, we win as we can profit from more sustainable economic opportunities that are not dependent upon a finite resource such as fossil fuel.

As a species we have the ability to change, adapt and choose our behaviour. Our colonisation of the world tells us so. What is required is the will to do so. Traditionally the will to change has arisen as an instinctive response to short-term threat or reward. These cannot continue to be our only motivations. We also need to respond to longer-term threats and rewards. By understanding that immediate responses are generated by instinct, we can better choose actions that satisfy those instincts, while being in the long-term best interests of ourselves and our descendants.

www.ingramcontent.com/pod-product-compliance
Lightning Source LLC
Chambersburg PA
CBHW020246290526
45784CB00003B/1126